GAYLORD F

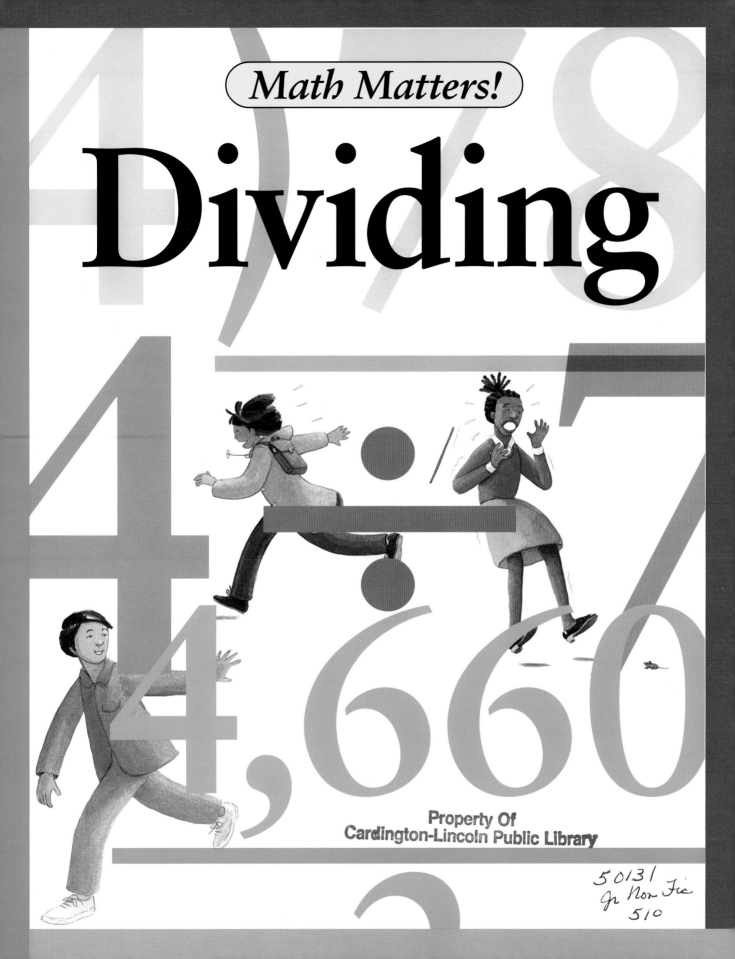

Math Matters!

Dividing

Look out for these sections to help you learn more about each topic:

Remember…

This provides a summary of the key concept(s) on each two-page entry. Use it to revise what you have learned.

Word check

These are new and important words that help you understand the ideas presented on each two-page entry.

All of the word check entries in this book are shown in the glossary on page 45. The versions in the glossary are sometimes more extensive explanations.

Book link…

Although this book can be used on its own, other titles in the *Math Matters!* set may provide more information on certain topics. This section tells you which other titles to refer to.

Place value

To make it easy for you to see exactly what we are doing, you will find colored columns behind the numbers in all the examples on this and the following pages. This is what the colors mean:

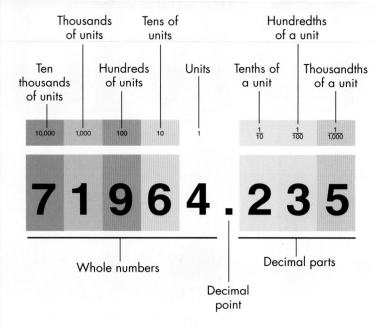

Whole numbers

Decimal parts

Decimal point

Series concept by *Brian Knapp and Duncan McCrae*
Text contributed by *Brian Knapp and Colin Bass*
Design and production by *Duncan McCrae*
Illustrations of characters by *Nicolas Debon*
Digital illustrations by *David Woodroffe*
Other illustrations by *Peter Bull Art Studio*
Editing by *Lorna Gilbert and Barbara Carragher*
Layout by *Duncan McCrae and Mark Palmer*
Reprographics by *Global Colour*
Printed and bound by *LEGO SpA*

First Published in the United States in 1999 by Grolier Educational, Sherman Turnpike, Danbury, CT 06816

Copyright © 1999
Atlantic Europe Publishing Company Limited

Library of Congress Cataloging-in-Publication Data
Math Matters!
   p. cm.
   Includes indexes.
   Contents: v.1.Numbers — v.2.Adding — v.3.Subtracting — v.4.Multiplying — v.5.Dividing — v.6.Decimals — v.7.Fractions – v.8.Shape — v.9.Size — v.10.Tables and Charts — v.11.Grids and Graphs — v.12.Chance and Average — v.13.Mental Arithmetic
ISBN 0–7172–9294–0 (set: alk. paper). — ISBN 0–7172–9295–9 (v.1: alk. paper). — ISBN 0–7172–9296–7 (v.2: alk. paper). — ISBN 0–7172–9297–5 (v.3: alk. paper). — ISBN 0–7172–9298–3 (v.4: alk. paper). — ISBN 0–7172–9299–1 (v.5: alk. paper). — ISBN 0–7172–9300–9 (v.6: alk. paper). — ISBN 0–7172–9301–7 (v.7: alk. paper). — ISBN 0–7172–9302–5 (v.8: alk. paper). — ISBN 0–7172–9303–3 (v.9: alk. paper). — ISBN 0–7172–9304–1 (v.10: alk. paper). — ISBN 0–7172–9305–X (v.11: alk. paper). — ISBN 0–7172–9306–8 (v.12: alk. paper). — ISBN 0–7172–9307–6 (v.13: alk. paper).

   1. Mathematics — Juvenile literature. [1. Mathematics.] I. Grolier Educational Corporation.
QA40.5.M38   1998
510 — dc21   98–7404
                                                                        CIP
                                                                         AC

This book is manufactured from sustainable managed forests. For every tree cut down at least one more is planted.

Contents

Introduction

$$84 \div 7 = 12$$

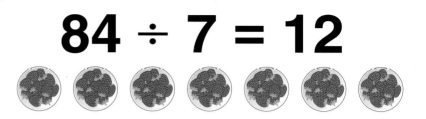

Dividing is something we do every day, often without realizing we are dividing. That is because we use other words. For example, we use the words "splitting up" or "cutting up" or "parts" or "on average." And many of the questions we ask ourselves are also dividing by another name. For example, we say "How many? What is the cost per liter? What is the price per gram? What is the speed? How many groups of something can I get out of …? How many can I afford? How long will it take?"

Dividing has only a few simple rules. There are also some basic division facts to learn and some smart

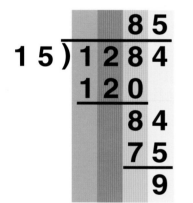

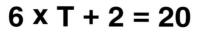

$$6 \times T + 2 = 20$$

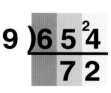

1:2

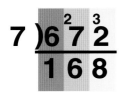

$$7\overline{)6\,7\,^{2}2^{3}}$$
$$1\,6\,8$$

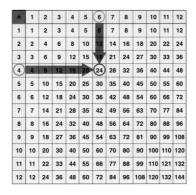

tricks that save time and allow us to check our answers.

What you will find is that by following this book with its step-by-step approach, it will be easy to learn the ideas of dividing. Since each idea is set out on a separate page, you can refer back quickly to an idea if you temporarily forget it.

As in all of the books in this mathematics set, there are many examples. They have been designed to be quite varied because you can use mathematics at any time, any place, anywhere. Some of the examples are based on fun stories, so have fun reading them as you go along.

$$783 \div 27 = ?$$

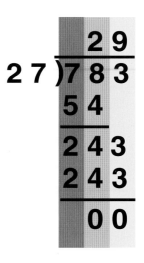

$$
\begin{array}{r}
2\,9 \\
2\,7\,\overline{)7\,8\,3} \\
5\,4 \\
\hline
2\,4\,3 \\
2\,4\,3 \\
\hline
0\,0
\end{array}
$$

$$7\overline{)2\,8\,0}$$
$$4\,0$$

$$11 \div 4 = 2, \textbf{ remainder } 3$$

Why divide?

Division is simply a quick way of taking away, or subtracting, the same number again and again.

There are many ways that you can subtract things. Some are faster than others.

The example on the right uses subtraction to find out how many times 10 can be split into 2's.

Start with 10 and subtract 2 to get 8, then start with 8 and subtract 2 and so on until you come to 0.

Counting up the number of subtractions, we get 5; so simply by subtracting, we know that 10 can be split into 5 lots of 2.

$$10 - 2 = 8$$
$$8 - 2 = 6$$
$$6 - 2 = 4$$
$$4 - 2 = 2$$
$$2 - 2 = 0$$

Here is a similar problem that a jeweler tried to solve, also by subtracting.

The jeweler's problem

A jeweler buys a bag of 84 diamonds, all of equal size. He wants to make brooches that each use 7 diamonds in a gold mounting.

However, unless the jeweler knows how many gold mountings he will need, he is in danger of buying too many and wasting his money. Or he might buy too few and have to go back to the warehouse to buy more, so wasting his time.

The jeweler decides to divide up the diamonds into little piles, each containing 7 jewels. What he is doing is subtracting 7 jewels from the main collection and setting them aside. Then he subtracts 7 more from the remaining collection and sets those aside. And so on. Again and again he subtracts 7 diamonds from the pile until there are none left.

This takes him a long time. This is how he was working:

$$84 - 7 = 77$$
$$77 - 7 = 70$$
$$70 - 7 = 63$$
$$63 - 7 = 56$$
$$56 - 7 = 49$$
$$49 - 7 = 42$$
$$42 - 7 = 35$$
$$35 - 7 = 28$$
$$28 - 7 = 21$$
$$21 - 7 = 14$$
$$14 - 7 = 7$$
$$7 - 7 = 0$$

By subtracting 7 each time from the pile, he discovers – slowly – that he has enough stones to make **12** brooches.

The jeweler could have used a quicker way to solve his problem. You can find out how on pages 12 and 13.

Remember... When you repeat subtraction, you take away the same number time after time. Division is a short way of doing this, but only if the number you are subtracting is the same time after time.

Word check

Dividing: A quick way of separating a number into many equal parts.

Separating: Splitting up a collection into several parts.

Subtracting: A quick way of counting back to find out how many are left after you remove some.

Splitting up

Splitting up a collection of things is a way of dividing. It is especially useful when we want to make sure that we can split up a collection equally.

Splitting up the strawberries

Frank was very proud of the strawberries he grew. In summer he and his wife Elsie often had a bowl of them with cream while they were watching tennis on television. They were very fair about it. Elsie used to split up the strawberries equally for them into smaller bowls, saying: "One for you, one for me, one for you, one for me…" until they had enough – usually about twelve each.

One Sunday, Frank and Elsie's children came to tea bringing Frank's mother too. Since there would be seven people, Frank would need to pick more strawberries than usual. He didn't count them, he just picked what he thought would be enough. In fact, he happened to pick 84. But Elsie still split them up equally into seven smaller bowls in her usual way.

Luckily for Frank, there were just enough for her to do it equally, and each person had exactly 12 strawberries.

No need for luck

Frank had no need for luck; he could have worked out just what he needed before he went to pick the fruit. Splitting things up equally is one of the useful things you can do <u>quickly</u> using dividing, as you will see in this book.

Notice, however, that Elsie did not do this because she didn't use any mathematics in her splitting. So she did not know that the answer would be **12** strawberries. To see this, she would have had to use multiplication facts backward, which is what division is all about, as you will see on page 10.

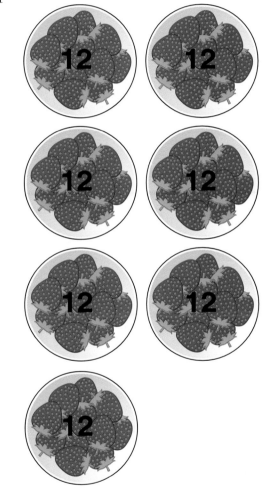

Remember... Splitting up equally is separating – or dividing – a number into many equal parts. So it is a form of division.

Also... If you know your multiplication facts, you will have spotted that 12 × 7 = 84.

This is why Elsie found she had **12** strawberries in each bowl when she began to divide them up.

There is more about the relationship between multiplying and dividing on page 16.

Word check

Multiplication facts: The numbers produced by multiplying together numbers we use a lot, such as 3 × 4 = 12. They are facts we remember rather than work out each time. Some people also refer to these multiplication facts as multiplication tables.

How division works

On this page we use a model to help show how division works.

The model we will use consists of small squares. Each individual square stands for **1** unit, and a group of **10** squares in a column stands for **10** units. You can see this on the right.

This is a shape for 10. Some people call this a <u>long</u>. 10 of these make a flat.

This is a shape for 1. It can also be called a <u>unit</u>. 10 of these make a long.

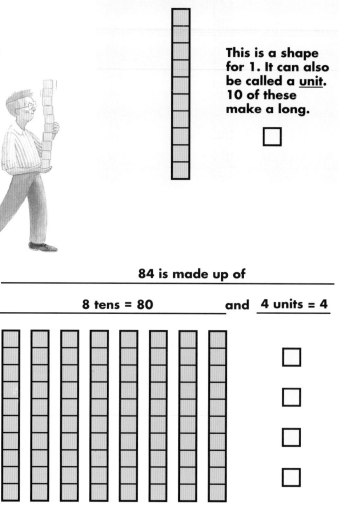

Let's start by working out **84** divided by **7**, since we already know the answer (see page 8). To start with, the number **84** contains 8 tens (8 longs) and 4 units, as shown using the model on the right.

Tens of units	Units
8	**4**

84 is made up of

8 tens = 80	and	4 units = 4

When we divide **84** by **7**, we are trying to split up **84** into 7 equal amounts.

Since 84 contains both tens and units, it makes sense first of all to split up the tens equally as far as we can.

We split up 7 tens, giving **1** ten to each portion, but then we have the last ten and 4 units left over.

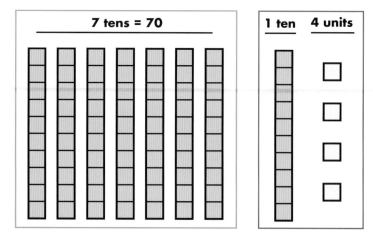

7 tens = 70

1 ten   **4 units**

1 ten is also 10 units   **4 units**

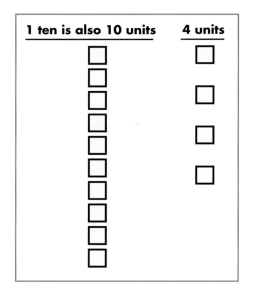

To go any further, we must separate, or regroup, this last ten as **10** units. Together with the **4** units we haven't yet split up, this makes **14** units.

7 equal groups of 2

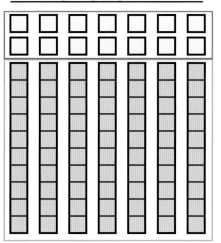

These **14** units can now be divided into **7** equal amounts.

Because we know the multiplication fact **7 × 2 = 14**, we know that **7** groups of **2** units uses up all **14** units.

7 equal groups of 12

So each equal amount gets **1** ten and **2** units, which, of course, we call **12**.

The model helps us see that **84** divided into **7** makes **7** equal amounts of **12**.

Written mathematically, this is:

$$84 \div 7 = 12$$

What we need to split up   How many groups   What each group is

Word check

÷ : A symbol for dividing. We say it "divided by." It is an alternative to ∕.

Flat: A large square representing 100. It can also be made up of ten "longs" put side by side.

Long: A long shape representing 10.

Regrouping: This means turning a long into ten units or a flat into ten longs.

Unit: A small, square shape representing 1.

Short division

If you want to divide by a number smaller than **10**, you use a method called short division. This is how it works.

As an example we will use the same calculation as on the previous page: **84** divided by 7. You can then compare the short division method with the model method we used on page 10.

The number we need to split up

Groups

$$84 \div 7 = ?$$

Division symbol

The answer we are going to work out

For short division we begin by writing the groups (**7**) and the total (**84**) side by side.

A parenthesis is placed between the two numbers and a line put below the number we need to split up. The answer will go below the line.

Notice that we have used colored columns to help us separate the tens from the units. For an explanation of what the colored columns mean, see page 2.

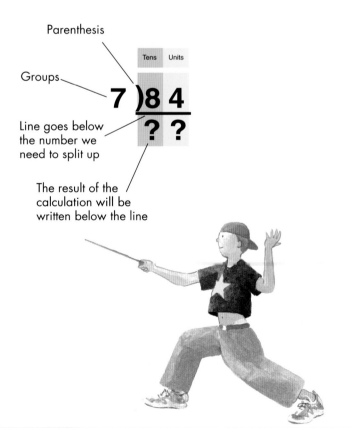

Parenthesis

Tens   Units

Groups

7)8 4

Line goes below the number we need to split up

The result of the calculation will be written below the line

Step 1: We start from the left, writing the answers below each number in turn.

First we ask, "How many times can we take 7 out of 8 (tens)?"
The answer is 1.
Show this by writing 1 below the 8 in the <u>tens</u> column.
This leaves 1 (ten) unsplit.

Unsplit 10

Step 2: Now we need to use this unsplit 10 by writing a <u>small</u> 1 next to the 4, leaving 14 units to be split up.

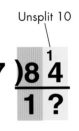

Step 3: Now we ask: "How many times can we take 7 out of 14 (units)?" The answer is 2.

Write this below the 4 in the units column.

This time there is nothing left unsplit, so the calculation is complete.

The answer, 12, is read from the bottom line.

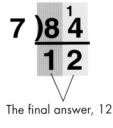

The final answer, 12

Remember: To write down numbers for short division, put the number you are dividing with first, then a parenthesis, then the number you are dividing <u>into</u>. Then start dividing from the left.

Word check

Short division: The way of writing down division by a number less than 10. The answer is written below the line, and the work is done in your head.

More short division

Short division can be used on large numbers provided you are still dividing by a number less than **10**. Here is an example.

We want to find the answer to this equation: How many amounts of 4 can we get from a total of 672?

$$672 \div 4 = ?$$

Step 1: The number 672 is made of 6 hundreds plus 7 tens and 2 units. We are dividing it by 4. Put the 4, then a parenthesis, then 672. Draw a horizontal line below this number.

100 10 1

4)6 7 2
  ? ? ?

Step 2: Now we begin by dividing 4 into the 6 (hundreds). It will only go once, leaving 2 (hundreds) unsplit. Put the answer 1 <u>below</u> the 6 in the hundreds column.

4)6 7 2
  1 ? ?

The unsplit 2 from the 100's column.

Step 3: We have 2 (hundreds) unsplit. Combine the 2 (hundreds) with the 7 (tens), placing a small 2 beside the next number, 7.

4)6 ²7 2
  1 ? ?

Step 4: We now work our way <u>right</u>, one number at a time. Next we have 27 (tens) to divide into 4 equal groups. Divide 4 into 27, which goes six times (6 × 4 = 24) and leaves 3 unsplit. Write the 6 below the tens column, and combine the 3 tens with the units.

7)6 7² 2³
  1 6 ?

Step 5: Now we work one place right again, into the units column. We have 32 units to be divided into 4 equal groups. The answer is 8 exactly. Place 8 under the 2.

7)6 7² 2³
  1 6 8 —— The final answer, 168

The final answer, **168**, is read from the bottom line.

672 ÷ 4 = 168

Remember... Draw a line under the larger number, and divide from left to right. Put the answers below the line.

Word check

Equation: A number sentence using the = symbol, telling us that two different ways of writing a number are the same. For example, 2 + 2 = 4 and 9 − 5 = 4, or 6 ÷ 2 = 3.

Division and multiplication

The previous pages have shown you that division and multiplication are very closely related. Actually, there are two division facts connected with each multiplication fact. As a result we can use a multiplication square to do a division calculation.

Using a multiplication square

You can make use of a multiplication square to divide because division is multiplication backward.

Let's take the multiplication fact that we have used on the previous pages again:

$$7 \times 12 = 84$$

We know that 84 split up equally 7 times makes 12.

Using ÷ as the symbol for "divided by" and = for "makes," this word sentence can be written as an equation:

$$84 \div 7 = 12$$

See how the numbers have changed sides from the multiplication equation?

We can look at the numbers in yet another way:

$$84 \div 12 = 7$$

Each multiplication fact has two division facts connected to it. The number square at the top of the opposite page shows this clearly.

×	1	2	3	4	5	6	7	8	9	10	11	12
1	1	2	3	4	5	6	7	8	9	10	11	12
2	2	4	6	8	10	12	14	16	18	20	22	24
3	3	6	9	12	15	18	21	24	27	30	33	36
4	4	8	12	16	20	24	28	32	36	40	44	48
5	5	10	15	20	25	30	35	40	45	50	55	60
6	6	12	18	24	30	36	42	48	54	60	66	72
7	7	14	21	28	35	42	49	56	63	70	77	84
8	8	16	24	32	40	48	56	64	72	80	88	96
9	9	18	27	36	45	54	63	72	81	90	99	108
10	10	20	30	40	50	60	70	80	90	100	110	120
11	11	22	33	44	55	66	77	88	99	110	121	132
12	12	24	36	48	60	72	84	96	108	120	132	144

Division fact 2
84 ÷ 12 = 7

Multiplication fact
7 × 12 = 84

Here is another example: The multiplication fact 4 × 6 = 24 is connected to the 2 division facts 24 ÷ 6 = 4 and 24 ÷ 4 = 6.

Division fact 1
24 ÷ 6 = 4

×	1	2	3	4	5	6	7	8	9	10	11	12
1	1	2	3	4	5	6	7	8	9	10	11	12
2	2	4	6	8	10	12	14	16	18	20	22	24
3	3	6	9	12	15	18	21	24	27	30	33	36
4	4	8	12	16	20	24	28	32	36	40	44	48
5	5	10	15	20	25	30	35	40	45	50	55	60
6	6	12	18	24	30	36	42	48	54	60	66	72
7	7	14	21	28	35	42	49	56	63	70	77	84
8	8	16	24	32	40	48	56	64	72	80	88	96
9	9	18	27	36	45	54	63	72	81	90	99	108
10	10	20	30	40	50	60	70	80	90	100	110	120
11	11	22	33	44	55	66	77	88	99	110	121	132
12	12	24	36	48	60	72	84	96	108	120	132	144

Division fact 2
24 ÷ 4 = 6

Multiplication fact
4 × 6 = 24

Remember... Every multiplication fact is connected to two division facts simply by rearranging the equation.

Word check

Division facts: The numbers produced by dividing numbers we use a lot, such as 6 ÷ 2 = 3. They are facts we remember rather than work out each time.

Fact family: A group of related facts about adding and subtracting or about multiplying and dividing.

Number square: A pattern of consecutive numbers arranged into a square grid.

Long division

Long division is simply another way of dividing when the number you are dividing by is bigger than **10**.

It is called <u>long</u> division because it makes more space for your work, and this makes it helpful when the numbers are too big for easy mental arithmetic.

Suppose we have to divide 783 by 27.

Step 1: Write down the numbers as shown here. It is much the same as for short division, but notice that the line goes <u>above</u> the number and the answer builds on top of that. This is because the space underneath is needed for your work.

Step 2: Start on the left.
How many times can we divide **27** into 7? Answer **0**, because **27** is bigger than 7. We do not need to write this **0** down and instead leave a blank.

Step 3: Divide **27** into the first two numbers (78). Answer **2**. Write this above the **8** because it is a number of tens.

This calculation was probably not easy to do in your head. Most people use a piece of scrap paper to work it out (2 × 27 = 54).

Write the 54 below the 78, and take it away. Was there anything left unsplit? Answer, yes, 24 tens. Draw a line then write the 24 below the line.

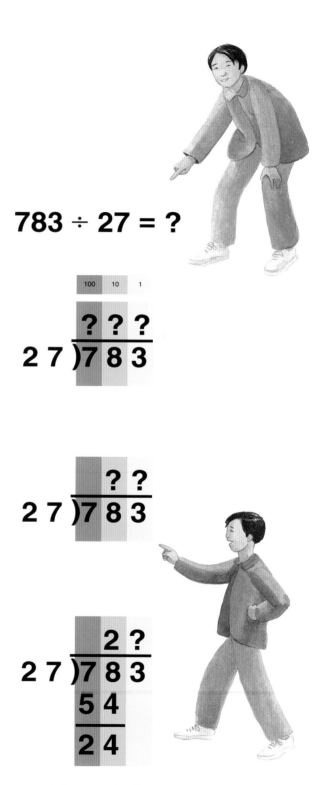

$$783 \div 27 = ?$$

Tip... To divide 27 into 78, work out 1 × 27 = 27, 2 × 27 = 54, 3 × 27 = 81, until you have gone one step too far.

Step 4: Bring down the next number.

Slide the **3** down its column to the same line as the remaining **24** tens to make **243**. This is what remains to be split up.

$$\begin{array}{r} 2\,9 \\ 2\,7\,)\overline{7\,8\,3} \\ 5\,4 \\ \hline 2\,4\,3 \end{array}$$

Step 5: Divide again.

How many times can we get **27** out of **243**?

Write **9** at the top, above the **3**, in the units column, because these are the **9** extra units given to each group.

$$\begin{array}{r} 2\,9 \\ 2\,7\,)\overline{7\,8\,3} \\ 5\,4 \\ \hline 2\,4\,3 \\ 2\,4\,3 \\ \hline 0\,0 \end{array}$$

Rough working... It is easy to see that $10 \times 27 = 270$ (just add a 0 to 27). This is slightly too big, so try **9**. $9 \times 27 = 243$ exactly.

Step 6: Was there anything left unsplit? Answer, no. This is the end of the calculation. The answer is **29**.

$783 \div 27 = 29$

Remember... Short division and long division are just the same. They are simply different ways of writing down division.

Word check

Long division: The way of writing down division by a number more than 10. The answer is written above the line, and the work is written in long columns down the page.

Will it divide exactly?

When we are deciding which division method to use, it is often helpful to know in advance whether the division will work out exactly, or whether there will be some left over. If it will work out exactly, we can often use short division or do the sum in our heads. If it won't go exactly, we might have to use a calculator or do it by long division if there is no calculator handy.

Here are some easy tests to find out.

2 If a number divides by 2, its last digit divides by 2. **Example:** 14; the last digit is 4, and 4 ÷ 2 = 2, so 14 divides by 2.

4 If a number divides by 4, the number formed by its last two digits divides by 4. **Example:** 1,520; the last two digits are 20, and 20 ÷ 4 = 5, so 1,520 divides by 4.

5 If a number divides by 5, its last digit is 5 or 0. **Example:** 70 ends in a 0 and 695 ends in a 5, so they both divide by 5.

8 If a number divides by 8, the number formed by its last three digits divides by 8. **Example:** 6,128; the last three digits are 128, and 128 ÷ 8 = 16, so 6,128 divides by 8.

10 If a number divides by 10, its last digit is 0. **Example:** The number 3,420 ends in a 0 and so divides by 10.

3 If a number divides by 3, the sum of its digits divides by 3.
Example: 7,125; the sum of the digits is 7 + 1 + 2 + 5 = 15, and 15 ÷ 3 = 5, so 7,125 divides by 3.

9 If a number divides by 9, the sum of its digits divides by 9.
Example: 7,128; the sum of the digits is 7 + 1 + 2 + 8 = 18, and 18 ÷ 9 = 2, so 7,128 divides by 9.

6 If a number divides by 6, it passes the tests for both 2 and 3.
Example: 7,122; test for 2: last digit 2 ÷ 2 = 1; <u>and</u> test for 3: 7 + 1 + 2 + 2 = 12; 12 ÷ 3 = 4, so 7,122 divides by 6.

12 If a number divides by 12, it passes the tests for both 4 and 3.
Example: 7,128; test for 4: last two digits 28 ÷ 4 = 7; <u>and</u> test for 3: 7 + 1 + 2 + 8 = 18; 18 ÷ 3 = 6, so 7,128 divides by 12.

Word check
Digit: The numerals 1, 2, 3, 4, 5, 6, 7, 8, 9, or 0. Several may be used to stand for a larger number. They are called digits to make it clear that they are only part of a complete number.

Short division with a remainder

When division leaves something over, the amount left over is called a remainder.

Suppose we want to divide 78 by 4.

$$78 \div 4 = ?$$

Step 1: We will use short division because we are dividing by a number smaller than 10.

   The number 78 is made up of 7 tens and 8 units.

   Find out how many times you can get 4 out of 7. Put the answer 1 below the 7. There is a remainder to carry forward of 3.

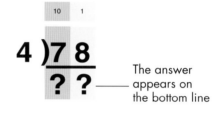

The answer appears on the bottom line

Step 2: The 3 left over is in the tens column, so it is worth 30 units. This, together with the 8 we haven't used yet, can be combined into 30 + 8 = 38 to be split up.

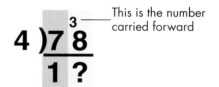

This is the number carried forward

Step 3: How many times can you get 4 out of 38? Answer 9 times, because 4 × 9 = 36. Put the 9 below the 38. Now there is just 2 left over. We cannot split 2 up equally between 4. The left-over amount is called the remainder.

remainder 2

Another example: What is the remainder when you divide 654 by 9?

$$654 \div 9 = ?$$

Step 1: Divide 9 into 6. It won't go. Carry the 6 to the right.

Step 2: Divide 9 into 65 (9 × 7 = 63). Put 7 below the 5. Carry the remainder of 2 to the right.

Step 3: Divide 9 into 24 (9 × 2 = 18). Put 2 below the 4. The remainder is 6.

So the answer is 72, remainder 6. This can be written as the mixed number 72 6/9 and simplified to 72 2/3.

Book link... For more information on mixed numbers, see page 36 of this book and the book *Fractions* in the *Math Matters!* set.

Remember... A remainder occurs in division when the original number cannot be split up equally.

Word check
Remainder: The number left over at the end of a division when the amount to be split up equally could not be split up completely.

Long division with a remainder

This method is very similar to the long division done on page 18. There are two differences. Here, there is a **0** and a remainder in the question.

What is the result of dividing **803** by **27**?

$803 \div 27 = ?$

Step 1: Write down the division as on page 18. How many times can we get **27** out of **8**? Answer **0**, because **27** is greater than **8**.

Step 2: Use the first two digits of **803** instead.

How many times can we get **27** out of **80**? Answer **2** ($2 \times 27 = 54$). Write this above the **0**, because it is a number of tens.

Write the **54** below the **80**, and take it away, because **54** tens have been taken from the **80** tens we started with.

Was there anything left insplit? We work out $80 - 54 = 26$.

So the answer is yes, **26** tens are left unsplit. Write **26** below the **54**.

Step 3: Slide the **3** down the units column to the same line as the **26** tens to make the **263** units remaining to be split up.

Step 4: How many times can we get 27 out of 263?

Answer 9, because 9 × 27 = 243. Write this 9 at the top, above the 3, in the units column.

Step 5: Write the 243 below the 263. Now take away. Remainder 20.

Step 6: Finally, we write, 803 divides by 27 29 times and leaves a remainder of 20.

803 ÷ 27 = 29
remainder 20

Remember... There is often a remainder after a long division. This remainder could be written as a fraction, which in this example would be ²⁰⁄₂₇. The remainder could also be written as a decimal.

Book link... Find out more about fractions in the book *Fractions* in the *Math Matters!* set. You can also find out more about decimals in the book *Decimals* in the *Math Matters!* set.

Division with decimal numbers

Many numbers we work with are not whole numbers, but decimal numbers. That is, they are whole numbers <u>and</u> parts of whole numbers. The parts of a number are to the right of the decimal point.

It is much easier to divide by a whole number than by a decimal, so we arrange things to make the number we are dividing by into a whole number.

Suppose we want to divide 28 by 0.7.

$$28 \div 0.7 = ?$$

The 0.7 is a decimal number. We want to make 0.7 a whole number, so we multiply 0.7 by 10: $0.7 \times 10 = 7$.

To balance this change, we also have to multiply 28 by 10: $28 \times 10 = 280$.

So the new division is 280 divided by 7.

$$280 \div 7 = ?$$

Now we can use short division:

Step 1: Write the short division out as shown on the right.

100	10	1
7)2	8	0
?	?	?

Step 2: Divide 7 into 2. This won't go. Divide 7 into 28. This will go 4 times exactly. There is no remainder to carry.

7)2 8 0
    4 ?

Step 3: Bring down the final 0. The final answer is 40.

7)2 8 0
    4 0

Dividing decimals of different lengths

Sometimes the decimal numbers in a division have different lengths. For example: 547.96 ÷ 9.5. Multiply both numbers by the same number of 10's until the number you are dividing by is a whole number. Multiply both numbers by 10. This changes 9.5 to 95, a whole number and 547.96 to 5,479.6. Notice that the number we are dividing into is still a decimal number. However, this won't cause any trouble.

Step 1: Using long division, divide 95 into the first two digits (54). It won't go. Divide 95 into the first three digits (547). The answer is 5. Write 5 above the 7. Write the result (5 × 95 = 475) underneath 547 and take away. The remainder is 72.

Step 2: Slide the 9 down its column to add to the remainder. This gives 729. Divide 95 into 729. The answer is 7, remainder 64. Write 7 on the answer line above the 9.

Now place a decimal point on the answer line above the decimal point already present in the number 5,479.6

Step 3: Slide the 6 down its column to add to the remainder. This gives 646. Divide 95 into 646. Answer 6, remainder 76.

Step 4: There are no more numbers to slide down, so write a 0 at the end giving 760. Divide 95 into 760. The answer is 8 exactly (there is no remainder).

Remember... To divide whole numbers into decimals, you can use either short or long division.

$$547.96 \div 9.5 = ?$$

is the same as

$$5{,}479.6 \div 95 = ?$$

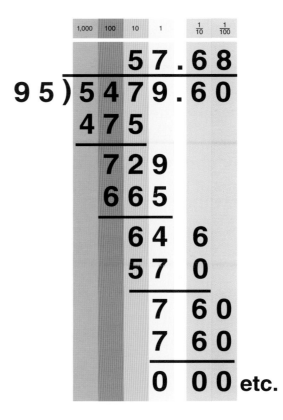

Word check
Digit: The numerals 1, 2, 3, 4, 5, 6, 7, 8, 9, or 0. Several may be used to stand for a larger number. They are called digits to make it clear that they are only part of a complete number.

When we cannot use a remainder

In the previous pages you have seen that division can often leave a remainder. So what do we do with the remainder? Here is an example that shows you how to think about the real meaning of a remainder.

The tramps and the boots

Four tramps go to an aid center, each hoping to be given a "new" pair of boots. As it happens, their feet are about the same size.

The center has six pairs of boots that will fit them reasonably well. So how does the center manager cope?

6 pairs of boots

Think about the problem

Six pairs of boots make 12 boots. Twelve boots shared among four tramps is three:

$$12 \div 4 = 3$$

This would use up all the boots, and each tramp could be given 3 boots. That would not be a useful calculation in this case since each tramp needs a <u>pair</u> of boots.

If the manager of the center did this, it would clearly be stupid. Nobody would benefit because none of the tramps could make use of the third boot.

Instead, the useful calculation is:

6 pairs of boots ÷ 4 tramps = 1 pair for each tramp and remainder 2 pairs (4 boots)

Remainder

Making sense of the remainder

It would be far more sensible for each tramp to receive one pair of boots, and for the center to keep the remaining two pairs of boots for future "clients."

This is an example of how division could produce a silly answer. It shows why you always have to look at answers with a commonsense view. And, by the way, most test graders give credit for common sense!

Remember... It is not enough just to do a calculation. The calculation is only useful if it gives a sensible answer. So always think what you are doing the calculation for and what use the remainder might be!

How to use a remainder

The idea of not being able to split something up equally is very common in division, but as you can see in these two examples, the remainder can sometimes be used sensibly. Here you will also see when the answer is best shown as a fraction.

The barbecue

George had a barbecue at home. His mom discovered that there were 4 vegetarians, and so they would each need three vegetarian burgers instead of the steaks that everyone else was eating.

Unfortunately, they only had 11 vegetarian burgers.

The problem they had to solve was how to <u>split</u> 11 <u>among</u> 4. In other words, they had to find out how many times can 4 be split out of 11? They got out the plates to find the answer and discovered that it was 2 each, but there were still 3 burgers remaining; that is, three were left over.

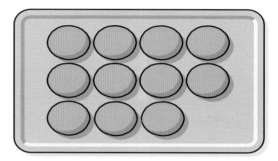

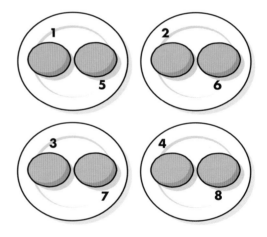

The remaining 3 burgers

What use is the remainder?

In this case it was best to use all the burgers, so they divided the remaining burgers among the guests (giving each an extra ¾), thus putting 2 + ¾ of a burger on each plate.

11 ÷ 4 = 2, remainder 3

The remainder can be written as $\frac{3}{4}$

Dividing and fractions... A fraction always contains a division. For example, if we write the fraction $\frac{1}{200}$, it is the same as writing 1 ÷ 200. See also page 34.

Thirsty play

Four friends were playing together in the garden one hot afternoon. The mother of one of them came out with a large jug of fruit juice that would fill **6** glasses.

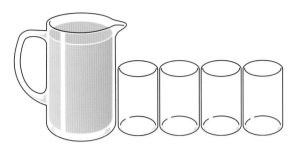

$$6 \div 4 = ?$$

She filled a glass for each child and put the partly empty jug on the table. This meant that there were **2** glasses-worth of juice remaining in the jug.

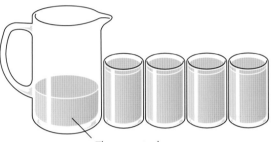

$$6 \div 4 = 1, \text{ remainder } 2$$

The remainder

The remainder can be written as ²⁄₄, which on dividing top and bottom by two becomes ½.

Splitting the remaining juice equally means that each of the friends receives the remainder as a very welcome half a glass worth.

Remainder 2 is $\frac{2}{4}$ or $\frac{1}{2}$

Remember... A remainder is often most sensibly expressed as a fraction. In these examples you will see that ¾ of a burger or ½ a glass is easy to split up.

Book link... Find out more about fractions in the book *Fractions* in the *Math Matters!* set.

Word check

Fraction: A special form of division using a numerator and denominator. The line between the two is called a dividing line.

Dividing to get value for money

Many stores sell goods in large bags or in multiple packs. But do you get better value with these than when you buy small packs or single items? Josh set out to investigate...

Josh was on a trip to Colombia, where coffee is grown. He wondered if he could save the family money by buying some of the large packs of coffee to take home.

Large coffee test

Coffee is sold by weight. One way to find out which size pack gives the best value is to calculate how much you pay for, say, 100 g. To do this you have to find the <u>price</u> and divide it by the <u>weight</u>.

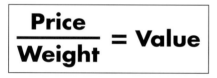

$$\frac{\text{Price}}{\text{Weight}} = \text{Value}$$

So Josh did this for two containers of coffee:

200 g of coffee (the small jar) cost **1,850** pesos, and 450 g of coffee (the large pack) cost **3,250** pesos.

To check which was better value, Josh needed to find out how much **100 g** of each cost.

First he calculated the cost of 100 g for the small jar:

Note: In Colombia the currency is the peso, but the currency sign has been left out of the calculations to make them easier to see.

$$100\,\text{g} \;\; \text{costs} \;\; \frac{1,850 \times 100}{200}$$

Which by short division is **925**

Josh now repeated the calculation for the cost of 100 g for the large pack:

Since **450 g costs 3,250**

so **100 g costs** $\dfrac{3,250 \times 100}{450}$

Which by long division is **722**

So the larger "economy" size cost 722 pesos per 100 g. This was a saving of 203 pesos per 100 g when compared with the small jar (925 − 722 = 203) and so was worth buying.

Multipack cola test

Josh found single bottles of cola and multipacks containing 6 bottles in the hotel shop:
6 bottle pack costs 1,050 pesos.
1 bottle costs 175 pesos.

Josh then needed to know how much each bottle in the multipack cost, so he divided the pack price by 6.

He found that:

$$\frac{1,050}{6} = 175$$

Each bottle in the pack cost 175 pesos, just the same as buying the cola bottles separately. In this case there was no advantage in buying the multipack.

Remember… You often need to know which item is the best value. To do this you have find out how much they cost for the same weight, size, etc.

Fractions, a special kind of division

Fractions are parts of a whole that use a horizontal line to show division.

We all go off to the zoo

The whole school is going on an outing by bus to the zoo. The bus company has big buses that can each take ¼ of the school and small buses that can each take ⅙ of the school.

On the day of the outing the bus company discovered it could only spare three big buses that day, though it had plenty of smaller ones. So how many buses should they provide?

They began thinking of three big buses and two small ones:

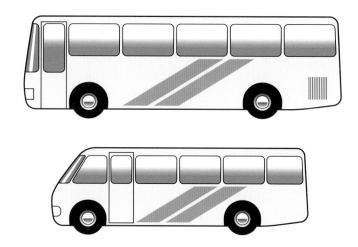

Three big buses would take $3 \times \dfrac{1}{4} = \dfrac{3}{4}$ of the school.

Two small buses would take $2 \times \dfrac{1}{6} = \dfrac{2}{6}$ of the school.

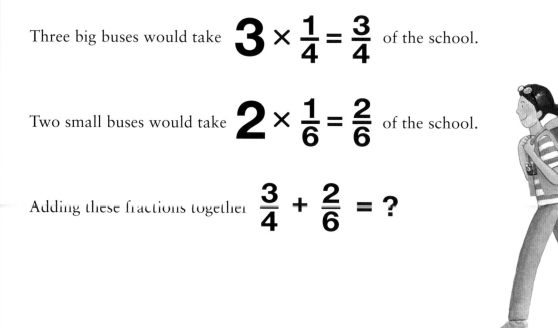

Adding these fractions together $\dfrac{3}{4} + \dfrac{2}{6} = ?$

To add fractions, the bottom numbers have to be the same. Since ¾ has a bottom number of **4**, and ⅖ has a bottom number of **6**, the easiest way to make the fractions the same kind is to convert them both to 24-ths, because 4 × 6 = 24.

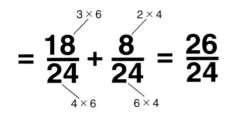

$$= \frac{18}{24} + \frac{8}{24} = \frac{26}{24}$$

The whole school is, of course, ²⁴⁄₂₄-ths. Since ¾ + ⅖ = ²⁶⁄₂₄, there would be empty seats this way. So would it help to use only two big buses and three small ones?

$$2 \times \frac{1}{4} + 3 \times \frac{1}{6}$$

$$= \frac{2}{4} + \frac{3}{6}$$

$$= \frac{12}{24} + \frac{12}{24}$$

$$= \frac{24}{24}$$

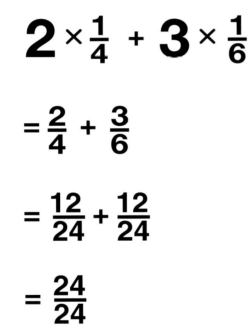

That takes exactly the right number of children.

Remember... To add fractions, the bottoms must be made the same. Once they are, just add the tops.

Book link... Find out more about fractions in the book *Fractions* in the *Math Matters!* set.

Word check

Dividing line: The line that separates the two number parts of a fraction. It is sometimes written horizontally, — and sometimes sloping, / . It is also called the division line. It is one of the signs we use for dividing. The other is ÷.

Fractions with the same value

Fractions can be written in several ways while having the same value.

For example, we write half of something as ½. It is actually 1 divided by 2. But a half is also the same as two quarters (¼, two divided by four).

Because these two fractions represent the same amount, we say that they are equivalent fractions (equivalent means "the same").

In this example notice that the numbers 2 and 4 both divide exactly by 2, so if you divide both the top and bottom of ¼ by 2, you get ½. This proves that ¼ has the same value as ½.

Equivalent fractions are very useful, as this example shows.

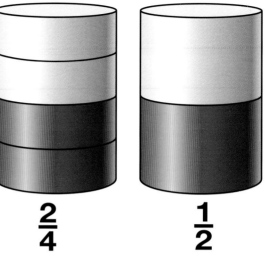

$$\frac{2}{4} \qquad \frac{1}{2}$$

$$\frac{2}{4} = \frac{1}{2}$$
$$2 \div 2 \qquad 4 \div 2$$

Making switches

In a factory making electrical switches the first-stage machine makes **15** pieces an hour. So each one takes ¹⁄₁₅-th of an hour. The second-stage machine works at only **12** pieces an hour. So each one takes ¹⁄₁₂-th of an hour.

This is how to work out how long it takes to make each switch.

The total time to make each switch is therefore ¹⁄₁₅-th + ¹⁄₁₂-th of an hour. So we need to work out:

$$\frac{1}{15} + \frac{1}{12} = ?$$

To add these fractions, we need to convert each fraction so that both are equivalent fractions, with the bottom numbers the same. We notice that both 15 and 12 will divide into 60, and so we now work out equivalent fractions.

$$\frac{1}{15} \text{ is the same as } \frac{4}{60}$$

(multiply the top and bottom by 4)

$$\frac{1}{12} \text{ is the same as } \frac{5}{60}$$

(multiply the top and bottom by 5). Now the fractions are equivalent (bottom numbers the same), so we can add them.

$$\frac{5}{60} + \frac{4}{60}$$

$$= \frac{5 + 4}{60}$$

$$= \frac{9}{60}$$

Each switch takes $\frac{9}{60}$-ths of an hour, or 9 minutes to be made.

Remember... Always look for the smallest number to use at the bottoms of the fractions. In this case both 12 and 15 go into 60. Similarly, if you had fractions with bottoms of 6 and 8, then you could use $6 \times 8 = 48$, but both numbers will also go into 24, and this is a smaller and so better number to work with.

Word check
Equivalent fractions: Fractions that have the same value.

Book link... Find out more about fractions in the book *Fractions* in the *Math Matters!* set.

Per, a word for divide

Per is a common shorthand meaning "for each" or "has already been divided."

For example, if a student receives an exam grade of **60** percent (written **60%**), it means that the teacher has worked out the grade as a fraction of **100** (**⁶⁰⁄₁₀₀**-ths). Here is another example.

Book link... Find out more about percentages in the book *Fractions* in the *Math Matters!* set.

Find out more about decimals in the book *Decimals*.

Can Marguerite get the job?

Marguerite had a challenge. She wanted to be the secretary to a manager of an office. This required that she be able to type **80** words per minute.

She worried that the manager might check her speed at an interview, so to be confident, she thought she would check it for herself.

She began to type at her keyboard. A friend timed her for fifteen minutes using her wristwatch. Marguerite then counted the number of words she had typed: 1,284.

Marguerite then used this number to work out her typing speed.

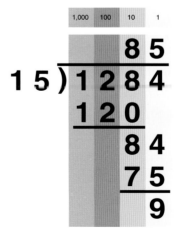

1,284 words in 15 minutes is

1,284 ÷ 15 words for each minute

or

$\frac{1,284}{15}$ **words per minute**

= 85 words per minute

Because she had proved that her typing speed was over **80** words per minute, she could apply for the job with more confidence.

```
                    8 5
        15)1 2 8 4
           1 2 0
                8 4
                7 5
                   9
```

| 1,000 | 100 | 10 | 1 |

Estimating before calculating

You will often use your calculator instead of long division in calculations, but how do you then know that you have the right answer? What happens if you accidentally entered a wrong number without realizing it? The way around the problem is to make a rough guess at the answer before you use the calculator. In fact, you should make this a rule before using the calculator for any calculation.

In this case Marguerite typed 1,284 words in 15 minutes, which is approximately 1,300 in 15 minutes. This is approximately 100 words per minute.

1,284 is approximately 1,300

1,300 ÷ 15 is approximately 100

Now that we have a rough estimate, we can compare it with a calculator.

Calculator work
1. Enter 1,284
2. Press division sign (÷ or /)
3. Enter 15
4. Press equals sign (=)
   (Answer reads 85.6)

What do we do with the remainder?

In this case there is a remainder. But Marguerite only wanted to know if she could type faster than **80** words per minute, so the remainder doesn't even have to be considered. So here again we have an example of looking at the answer in terms of our real needs.

Remember... In some cases the remainder is not important. Learn when to ignore it.

Word check
Percent: A number followed by the % symbol means the number is divided by 100. It is a way of writing a fraction.

The "in" word that means dividing

There are many ways in which dividing is used. In this case the word "in" is used to mean divide.

If you come to a steep hill, the chances are you see a warning sign that uses the word "in." This is a ratio. It is another way of writing "<u>up</u> divided by <u>along</u>."

There are many ways in which you can measure the steepness of a slope. One of them is to think of the slope as a kind of imaginary staircase.

This is
the slope

1 unit up

1 unit along

This is the
imaginary
staircase

The slope in the diagram on the right is matched by a staircase in which the length of the treads (1 unit) equals the height of the risers (1 unit). So for every step up or down the staircase, you go as far up or down as you do on the level.

This can be written down as

1 in 1

but it can also be written as

1:1 (a ratio)

It is also the fraction

$$\frac{1}{1}$$

In this example the slope has shallower steps, and you go along **2** units for every **1** you go up or down.

Here the slope is
1 in 2
or
1:2
or the fraction
$$\frac{1}{2}$$

1 unit up

2 units along

Here the slope is **2** up for every **6** along. So the slope is
2 in 6
Dividing through by **2** this simplifies to
1 in 3
or
1:3
or the fraction
$$\frac{1}{3}$$
This is even less steep.

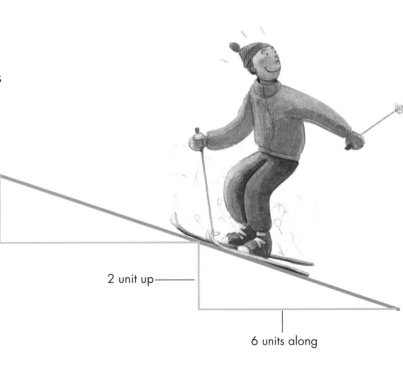

2 unit up

6 units along

Remember... These special forms of division replace the division line by the word "in" or a colon (:). That is why **1:2** is steeper than **1:3**.

Word check
Ratio: A method of comparing different numbers by placing them on either side of a colon (:); for example, 1:2. The numbers must be measured in the same units. The order of the numbers matters. A ratio is like a fraction.

Solving division equations

Many kinds of problems involve division. Here you can see how we use division to find an unknown amount in an equation.

The truffles

Kevin and Su are having a family gathering. Kevin has been out to buy 20 chocolate truffles to eat at the end of dinner. His elderly mother will want only two. The others will be shared equally among Kevin, Su, and their 4 friends.

Su does not know how many truffles each person will have. She works it out like this, using the letter T for the number of truffles per person.

Mother and 6 other friends came to dinner. Suppose everybody apart from Mother has T truffles.

We know that 6 (people) × T (truffles) + 2 (for mother) will eat the 20 truffles. This can be written as:

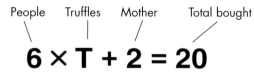

People   Truffles   Mother   Total bought

$$6 \times T + 2 = 20$$

So the problem is to find how many truffles T represents.

It is easier for Su to first rearrange the numbers. So she does this by subtracting 2 from both sides of the equation.

That makes

Remember, if you do the same to both sides of an equation, you don't change the equation.

$$6 \times T + 2 - 2 = 20 - 2$$

Now she has a simpler problem

$$6 \times T = 18$$

So she can now divide both sides by **6**. This will leave **T** on one side of the equation, and what is on the right will be the answer

$$\frac{6}{6} \times T = \frac{18}{6}$$

and since $\frac{6}{6} = 1$, this means 1T, or

$$T = \frac{18}{6}$$

and since $18 \div 6 = 3$,

$$T = 3$$

So everyone has **3** truffles, and Mother has **2**.

Remember... To check your answer. It is always worth looking for a way to check that the answer is correct. A good way is to put the answers back into the question to check that they work. Here, **6** people each take **3** truffles, making **18**. Mother takes **2**. So the total truffles = **20**, which is correct.

What symbols mean

Here is a list of the common math symbols together with an example of how they are used. You will find this list in each of the *Math Matters!* books, so that you can turn to any book if you want to look up the meaning of a symbol.

— Between two numbers this symbol means "subtract" or "minus." In front of one number it means the number is negative. In Latin *minus* means "less."

✚ The symbol for adding. We say it "plus." In Latin *plus* means "more."

✖ The symbol for multiplying. We say it "multiplied by" or "times."

= The symbol for equals. We say it "equals" or "makes." It comes from a Latin word meaning "level" because weighing scales are level when the amounts on each side are equal.

$$(8 + 9 - 3) \times \frac{2}{5} = 5.6$$

( ) Parentheses. You do everything inside the parentheses first. Parentheses always occur in pairs.

—, /, and **÷** Three symbols for dividing. We say it "divided by." A pair of numbers above and below a / or — make a fraction, so ²⁄₅ or $\frac{2}{5}$ is the fraction two-fifths.

■ This is a decimal point. It is a dot written after the units when a number contains parts of a unit as well as whole numbers. This is the decimal number five point six or five and six-tenths.

Glossary

Terms commonly used in this book.

Adding: A quick way of counting.

Denominator: The number written on the bottom of a fraction.

Digit: The numerals 1, 2, 3, 4, 5, 6, 7, 8, 9, or 0. Several may be used to stand for a larger number. They are called digits to make it clear that they are only part of a complete number. So we might say, "The second digit is 4," meaning the second numeral from the left. Or we might say, "That is a two-digit number," meaning that it has two numerals in it, tens and units.

Dividing: A quick way of separating a number into many equal parts.

Dividing line: The line that separates the two number parts of a fraction. It is sometimes written horizontally — and sometimes sloping /. It is also called the division line. It is one of the signs we use for dividing. The other is ÷.

Division facts: The numbers produced by dividing numbers we use a lot, such as 6 ÷ 2 = 3. They are facts we remember rather than work out each time. Division facts are the answers we work out backward from multiplication facts. *See* Multiplication facts.

Equation: A number sentence using the = symbol, telling us that two different ways of writing a number are the same. For example, 2 + 2 = 4 and 9 − 5 = 4, or 6 ÷ 2 = 3.

Equivalent fractions: Fractions that have the same value.

Fact family: A group of related facts about adding and subtracting or about multiplying and dividing.

Flat: A large square representing 100. It can also be made up of ten "longs" put side by side.

Fraction: A special form of division using a numerator and denominator. The line between the two is called a dividing line.

Long: A long shape representing 10.

Long division: The way of writing down division by a number more than 10. The answer is written above the line, and the work is written in long columns down the page.

Multiplication facts: The numbers produced by multiplying together numbers we use a lot, such as 3 × 4 = 12. They are facts we remember rather than work out each time. Some people also refer to these multiplication facts as multiplication tables.

Number square: A pattern of consecutive numbers arranged into a square grid.

Numerator: The number written on the top of a fraction.

Percent: A number followed by the % symbol means the number is divided by 100. It is a way of writing a fraction.

Ratio: A method of comparing different numbers by placing them on either side of a colon (:); for example, 1:2. The numbers must be measured in the same units. The order of the numbers matters. A ratio is like a fraction.

Regrouping: This means turning a long into ten units or a flat into ten longs.

Remainder: The number left over at the end of a division when the amount to be split up equally could not be split up completely.

Separating: Splitting up a collection into several parts.

Short division: The way of writing down division by a number less than 10. The answer is written below the line, and the work is done in your head.

Subtracting: A quick way of counting back to find out how many are left after you remove some.

Unit: 1 of something. A small square shape representing 1.

Set index